MORAY
EELS

MORAY
EELS

DON P. ROTHAUS

THE CHILD'S WORLD

As the divers descend toward the coral reef, they enter a world of color and beauty. Fish of all different shapes, sizes, and colors swim around the reef, schooling in and around its many valleys, cracks, and crevices. The divers begin a careful search, shining their lights underneath ledges, into the cracks and the small caves.

The lights reveal a number of fish and shrimp that use these hiding places to rest during the daylight hours. The divers' patience is finally rewarded when they find the subject of their search. Their lights sparkle off the long teeth of a large green moray, its body tucked far back within the recesses of the reef, its head swaying in the lazy current.

Morays are a small group of eel-shaped fishes found in tropical and subtropical oceans. They live around coral reefs and in rocky habitats at depths of five to 150 feet. There are nearly 100 species of moray, ranging in size from the *green moray*, ten feet in length, to the *pygmy moray*, as small as eight inches. Most moray eels are between four and five feet long. Morays may live to be twenty-five years old.

A typical moray eel has a long, ribbon-shaped body. A dorsal fin runs the entire length of its back. The moray's skin is thick, wrinkled, and leathery. Unlike most fish, moray eels do not have scales, but some are covered with a protective mucus. The moray's gill opening is small and round, and its teeth are long and sharp, convenient for grasping and holding fish.

The various species of moray eels around the world are easy to identify by their color, pattern, and size, and the area in which they are found. Some of the more common morays found near the United States are the green moray, the *spotted moray*, the *California moray*, the *chain moray*, and the *goldentail moray*.

The moray eel has an undeserved reputation as a vicious and dangerous animal. The eel must keep its mouth open almost all the time to allow water to pass over its gills. The eel's gaping mouth reveals many fanglike teeth. We normally interpret such a show of teeth as a threat, but the moray eel is actually quite shy.

There are a few situations that cause a moray to become aggressive. If a diver or fisherman injures or threatens a moray, it may bite to defend itself. Divers who unknowingly reach into a moray's hiding place, or *lair* may be in for a surprise; the moray eel, in defending its home, may bite! Finally, although morays enjoy being hand-fed by divers, on rare occasions they accidentally bite because of their poor eyesight and the excitement and competition that surrounds these free handouts.

The moray is a *nocturnal predator*, which means that it hunts at night. During the daylight hours it stays within the confines of its lair, but at night it ventures out in search of its prey. The moray eel has a keen sense of smell. The tube-shaped nostrils on the front of its snout help it locate its food. Almost all moray species eat a variety of small to medium-sized fish, and also prey on octopus, mussels, clams, lobsters, shrimp, and a variety of other shellfish. Occasionally, morays scavenge dead fish.

Morays use their fanglike teeth to catch and hold their prey. These teeth angle back toward the eel's throat, making it difficult for the captured animal to wiggle free. The moray often adjusts a captured fish in its mouth so that it swallows the head first. This keeps the sharp spines of the prey's dorsal fin from sticking into the moray's throat. The moray is also equipped with a set of platelike crushing teeth, known as *pharyngeal teeth*, used to crush the shells of clams, shrimp, crabs, and lobsters.

Moray eels have been prowling the oceans for millions of years. During fossil-collecting expeditions, scientists have found ancient moray teeth estimated to be nearly two million years old! Moray teeth have also been found in ancient Indian garbage mounds, known as *middens,* along the California coast.

After moray eels hatch from their eggs, they begin life as long, transparent, leaflike larvae. This larval stage is known as the *leptocephalus* stage. During this period, the larval morays float at the mercy of the ocean currents, feeding on microscopic animals and plants known as *plankton.* As the tiny animals grow they begin to take on the appearance of the adults. By the time they finally settle near a coral reef or rocky habitat, they are recognizable as juvenile morays.

Although the moray eel can be a dangerous preda-tor, there are two animals that have no fear of this crea-ture. The tiny fish known as the *cleaning wrasse* cruises around the face and body of the moray, feeding on par-asites. Another animal, the *cleaner shrimp*, wanders along the edge of the eel's mouth and teeth, providing its cleaning service. The moray benefits from both relation-ships by having annoying parasites removed from its

body, and the cleaning wrasse and cleaner shrimp benefit by receiving an easy meal. This kind of relationship is known as *symbiosis*, or *mutualism*.

Scuba divers around the world enjoy finding and feeding moray eels. In some areas morays have become so accustomed to divers that they eagerly come out of their lairs to greet them, hoping to be fed. Like our own pets, some of these morays have even been given names! It is important to realize, however, that these graceful animals are not pets. They are wild animals that may at times be unpredictable. As long as divers approach morays with respect, move slowly, and act gently, safe and rewarding interactions will continue to occur.

INDEX

PHOTO RESEARCH
Jim Rothaus / James R. Rothaus & Associates

PHOTO EDITOR
Robert A. Honey / Seattle

PHOTO CREDITS
Norbert Wu: front cover,
2,4,18,24
COMSTOCK: 7,8,28
INNERSPACE VISIONS / Doug Perrine:
11,17,21,22,31
Marty Snyderman: 13,27
Jeff Rotman: 14

Library of Congress Cataloging-in-Publication Data
Rothaus, Don
Moray eels / Don Rothaus.
p. cm.
Includes index.
ISBN 1-56766-187-4 (lib. Bdg.)
1. Morays – Juvenile literature
[1. Morays.] I. Title.
QL637.9.A5R68 1995   95-12144
597'.51 – dc20   CIP
                                                    AC